My Body Will Heal

For Anthony Jr. and Sarai —

I dedicate this book to you, my precious treasures,
in celebration of the remarkable harmony between
the mind, body, and soul. May you forever trust
in the innate healing power of your bodies and
the brilliance of your nervous systems to flourish.
Embrace the beauty of your interconnected existence
and always follow the symphony of your inner wisdom,
allowing your beings to resonate with vitality.

With boundless love,
Mama

Here we are, let's start the show;
The nervous system is the first place we'll go.
It starts with the brain,
Who's the master controller,
Then travels down pathways of nerves
In your body all over.

To the heart, the lungs, and even your skin,
To your belly, your muscles, and even your chin!
The brain sends messages to your body
Through vertebrae in your spine!
The nervous system controls
Every step along the assembly line.

From the brain to the spine, the message is clear,
So long as there's no interference in here.
Once the message arrives it's time to act quick,
for there's an important task to finish.
Back up to your brain in record time,
this important pathway is how our body heals in the nick of time.
You may be thinking, what else can our amazing body do?
Come along, let's go see, it was created to heal just for you …

You have two lungs that sit in your chest,
They expand like a balloon when you take a deep breath.
You can blow the air out like you blow out a candle.
It's called inhalation and exhalation,
two big words that have an importation rotation.

So where are these two lungs
That pump oxygen flowing to keep us alive?
They're protected by our ribs, hiding inside.

Taking deep breaths in and out of your nose
Really does the trick, especially when you're frustrated
And having a fit.
Breathing can calm you down and restore ease inside.
Breathing is the trick to healing your mind.

It's important to breathe air that is healthy and clean —
For our lungs are a filtering machine.

Next, we meet in the digestive tract,
That turns your food into poop like a magic act.
It starts with your mouth and ends with your rectum.
Your food travels quick with such great momentum.

It starts in the mouth, then to the esophagus,
Now to the stomach and onto both small and large intestines,
With great protection by our friends
The greater and lesser omentum.

This fast movement is called peristalsis.

The small intestine absorbs nutrients from your food,
While the large intestine takes in water to transform it.
Your digestive tract is a magical magician
That uses your nervous system to perform it.

That's right, your nervous system controls the show.
It's your brain and your gut that control your emotions, you know?

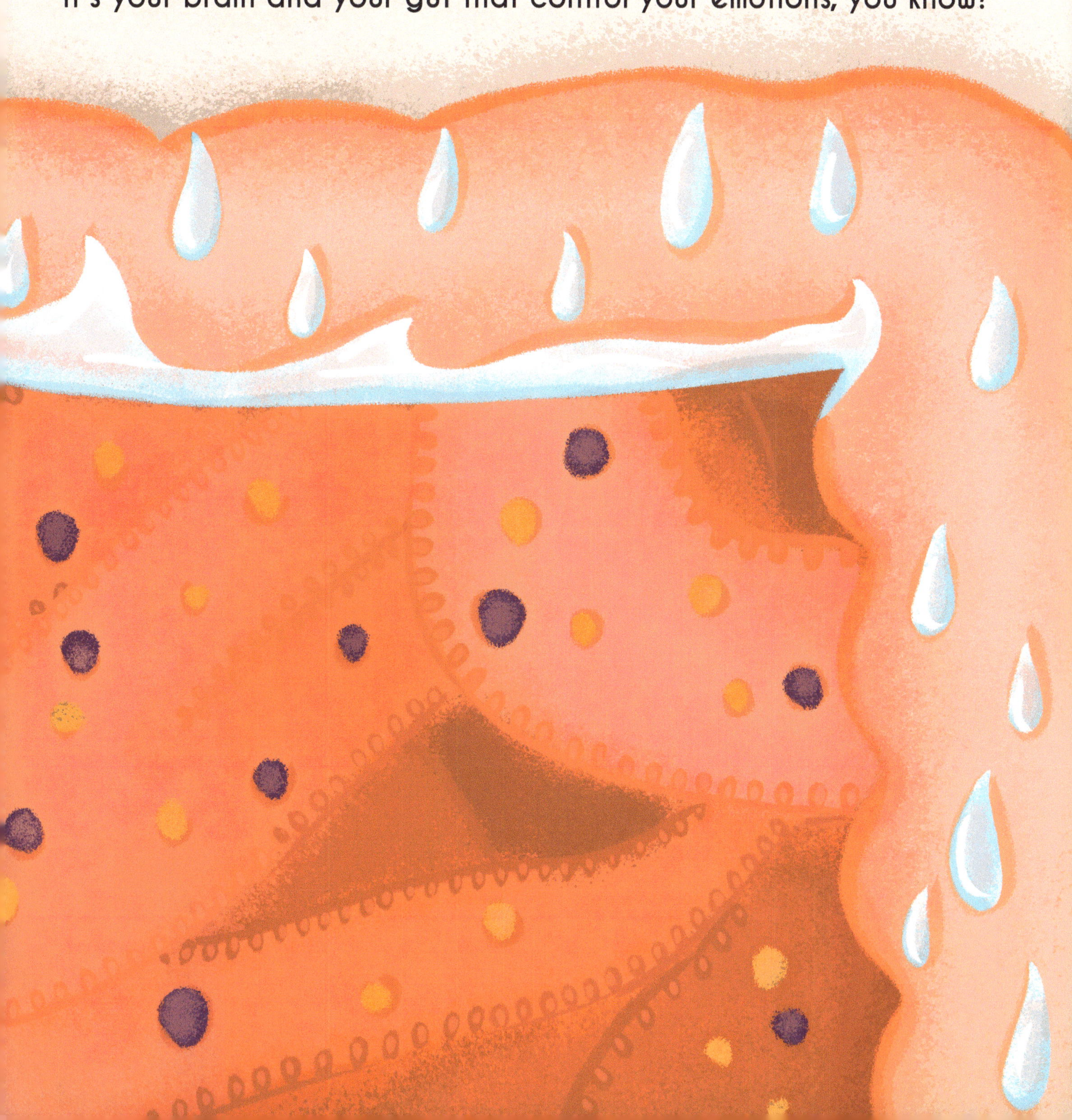

We better keep going, there's no time to quit,
Our endocrine system plays a big role in how we restore it.

From growing to sleeping among other things,
The endocrine system can really cause some swings.
We have neurotransmitters in our body
To communicate with our cells to tell them how to function well.

If our endocrine system is sluggish and slow,
Our body won't heal well and boy it will show.

When our endocrine system is up and running in tip top shape...
...our mood, our happiness and our hormones will celebrate.

We must keep going, there's so much to see,
Our next stop is the immune system,
Which keeps you healthy, you see!
Adaptation is the name of the game,
With the help of the thymus, white blood cells,
lymph system and even your spleen!

When your immune system is supported and strong,
You'll be adapting all the days long.
But when you're stressed and tired inside,
The immune system jumps off the adaptation ride.
You may feel sluggish and slow or sick and yucky;
That's why it's important to eat healthy fruits and vegetables
That fill up your tummy!

The immune system protects us
And keeps our body adapting on the inside,
From outside invaders that try to take us on
A nasty roller coaster ride.
So long as we're rested, eating healthy,
And our nervous system connection is flowing swell,
The immune system stays quiet helping us
Undercover to keep us well.

Last but not least, it's time for a ride,
Along the biggest and strongest organ
You see on the outside.
Our skin is an organ, yes, it is true!
It covers and protects us all the days through.

Our skin is a barrier between the inside and out,
Where you see bumps, bruises and scrapes
That heal quickly, without a doubt.

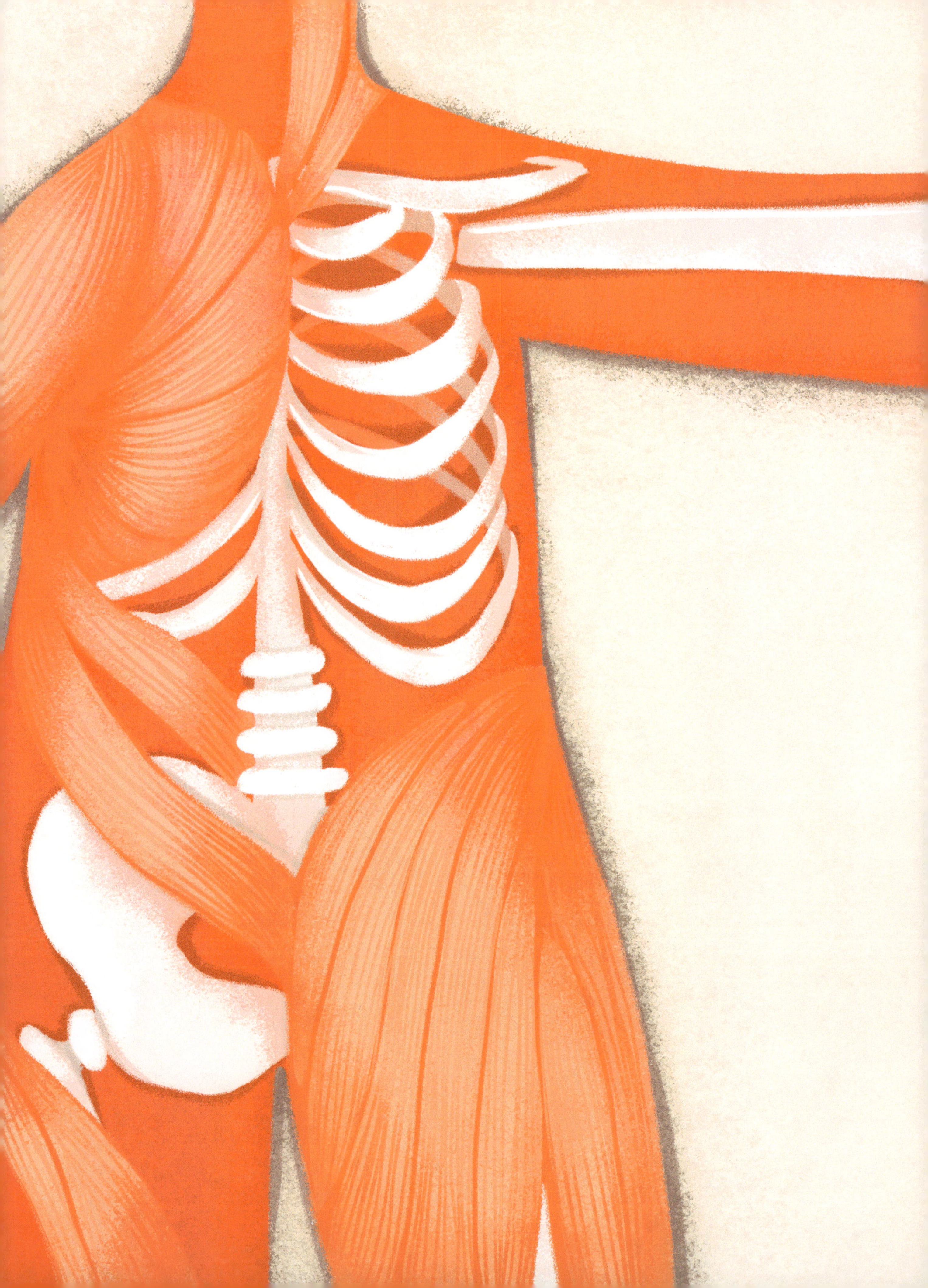

Under your skin are the bones that reside,
As the foundation and backbone for the muscles,
Tissues and organs keeping us alive!
We have many bones, 206 to be exact!

As you grow bigger it's important to build
Healthy bones and skin the natural way.
With protein from meats, raw dairy, eggs,
And several fruits and vegetable snacks throughout the day.

Your body is healthy, so strong and so wise.
You must take care of it for it to last you a long time.

By drinking water and sleeping and eating good food,
You will greatly affect your positive mood.

Before we finish it's important to know
You carry a special gift with you everywhere you go...
A gift of intelligence and a voice that's so wise,
A gift of healing potential and an opportunity to thrive.

By listening to this special voice that resides,
You will always honor your innate healing wisdom inside.
Listen to this voice often, as you were created to heal.
It's your own special superpower to take with you year after year.

www.ingramcontent.com/pod-product-compliance
Lightning Source LLC
Chambersburg PA
CBHW042124110726
48006CB00003B/753